COCKATIELS

Hamlyn
PET CARE
Handbooks

COCKATIELS

Dulcie and Freddie Cooke

HAMLYN

Published by
The Hamlyn Publishing Group Limited
a division of the Octopus Publishing Group plc
Michelin House, 81 Fulham Road
London SW3 6RB, England

First published 1988

ISBN 0 600 55749 9

Some of the material in this book
is reproduced from other books published
by The Hamlyn Publishing Group Limited

Printed by Mandarin Offset, Hong Kong

Contents

Introduction

The wild grey Cockatiel originated in Australia, where it is widely distributed except in the large conurbations and coastal areas. Living in bush and woodland, nesting in hollows in trees, it is found in large numbers wherever there is an abundance of food. Its diet is various seeds and includes nectar of eucalyptus blossoms. Cockatiels are fond of water, where they congregate in flocks, their yellow crests glinting in the sunlight, wading in shallow stretches of water by riversides.

With their attractive appearance combined with a friendly nature they became widely sought after as pets, and large numbers were exported to Europe and the USA from the middle of the nineteenth century until 1960, when the Australian government banned the sale of wild caught birds.

Being free breeders in captivity they soon became domesticated, and with the added attraction of an expanding range of beautiful colour mutations are now one of the most popular and sought after birds for cage and aviary. All over the world where birds are kept as pets the Cockatiel provides a delightful, affectionate, and often talkative pet.

To the owner and breeder of cockatiels in aviaries, these lovely birds mean many things: beauty, an absorbing interest and a hobby by which much is learnt about nature, nutrition and the general care of parrot-like birds. Above all, many lasting friendships are forged between owners through their common interests. This book is written mainly for newcomers to cockatiel keeping and is intended to provide some useful hints to the reader about this wonderful, challenging and absorbing pastime.

In the last few years many people have become the proud owners of pet Cockatiels, and many more have progressed from owners of a pet in the home to owners of an aviary as a feature and interest in their garden.

It is the custom now to use and enjoy the garden, if there is one, much more than years ago. Barbecue

*Pair of grey cockatiels as
they appear in the wild in
Australia. They are by
nature very gregarious*

equipment, lounger chairs, tables for serving food outdoors, all abound in almost every town and supermarket in the country. What better way to add still further to the interest and attractions of the garden than to add an aviary large enough for two pairs of Cockatiels. Those wonderful little characters will make sure there is always something of interest to watch and enjoy.

New friendships will no doubt be made through the birds, and new horizons opened through this wonderful pastime of birdkeeping.

Colours
and mutations

Normal

This is the domesticated counterpart of the wild grey bird. The feather colours vary from grey to charcoal and there is a white band along the front of the wings. The distinctive features are the crest which, when held erect, can be up to 75 mm (3 inches) high, and the bright orange-red cheek patches.

In the nest the young look alike, but as they moult out from three months onwards the sex becomes obvious. When adult the cock has a yellow crest and a more brilliant looking cheek patch as primrose yellow runs through the forehead and into the crest. The cheeks are also yellow with a suffusion of white surrounding the rear and below the cheek patch. The tail feathers can be very dark and do not have any markings underneath. The hen's cheek patches appear to be duller as they are surrounded by grey, there can be a ring of whitish-grey feathers around the eye and the crest is grey, often with a mottled appearance. A hen has spots underneath her flight feathers, and a cock does not, but the major feather difference is in the tail, as the outer feathers of the hen's are yellow and underneath all are striped.

Mutations

The different colours that have appeared are due to defects in the bird's genetic make up, which has affected its body chemistry, and is known as a mutation of the genes which produces colour. This rarely occurs in the wild and when it does the survival rate is very low.

It was only after nearly 100 years of being bred in captivity that the first new colour or mutation, Pied, was reported from Europe. This was most likely to have

Lutino and Cinnamon Pearl Pied Cockatiels

been due to inbreeding, and as the majority of Cockatiels were being kept in the USA it is not surprising that many of the new colour mutations have since arisen there. When a new colour is discovered it is a lengthy and costly process to establish a healthy strain to a good standard. After many years of breeding, the shortness of legs and lack of size is still to be noticed in a number of mutations.

Splits is a term used to describe birds that carry unseen another colour or colours, which are capable of being passed on to offspring.

The sex-linked mutation colours, for which only cocks can be split, are Lutino, Pearl and Cinnamon. Recessive mutation colours, for which both cocks and hens can be split, are Fallow, Pied and Whitefaced. An example of a split shown in print is Normal/Lutino, which means that Normal is the colour that is visible, Lutino being the hidden colour.

Lutino

This is the correct name for all-white Cockatiels. The colour of these birds varies from white to a deep primrose yellow. With age some birds develop a light lavender wash down the back. It is the more yellow

Lutino Cockatiel

looking birds that are most sought after. Lutino chicks have red eyes with pink feet. Many carry a genetic fault, passed on since this mutation was found in the USA in 1958: a small clear patch at the back of the head, which is inherited baldness. Do not reject an otherwise nice bird for this reason, or accept feather plucking or over preening as the cause.

A normal cock mated to a Lutino hen will produce all Normal looking young: the cock chicks will be split for Lutino and the hens, which cannot be split, will be Normal.

A Lutino cock mated to a Normal hen will produce Normal cocks all split for Lutino and all Lutino hens.

When sexing the young of Lutino mated to Lutino, wing spots and tail stripes are not always a sure guide to a hen. Hens might sing for a short time, but once cocks start they sing constantly, which is the best indication.

Pearl

These birds have standard orange cheek patches, their faces are yellow flecked with grey, and the yellow crests are streaked. The tail is streaked yellow, but the outstanding effect is the pearling on the back of the neck carrying on down the shoulders and back, with the breast often carrying a similar effect. The pearling on the feathers is round to oval, white or yellow, edged with charcoal grey, giving the scalloped or pearl appearance. There is a clear band along the front of the wings and the flight feathers are two-coloured, appearing dark grey at the ends. The undersides of the wings are spotted and mottled.

Lacewings

These are the same as Pearls except that the scalloped feathers are elongated (oval), and the result of selected breeding. There are large variations in colour from white, to silvery, to deep gold pearling. Cocks and hens look the same until they moult. When this happens the hens retain their beautiful markings, but the cocks revert to birds of normal appearance, very often to a much darker charcoal colour, almost black, making sexing straightforward.

Cinnamon Pied

Cinnamon Pearl

Cinnamon
Pearl Pied

Pearl Pied

Pearl

Cinnamon

Lutino

*Pair of Cinnamon
Cockatiels*

Cinnamon

This sex-linked mutation came in the 1960s from
Europe, where it was called Isabella. Both cocks and
hens have similar markings to Normals with the grey
colour replaced by brown (Cinnamon). The very young
have pale reddish eyes and pinkish feet and legs. The
Cinnamon colour varies from light to dark, and they are
sexed the same as Normals.

Fallow

This recessive mutation was discovered in the USA in the early 1970s, and although common there, very few are bred in the UK. The reason may be that it is very like the sex-linked Cinnamon, but has red eyes and the colour is paler and variable, often two-toned, diffused with primrose and with a yellow face. The hens are often much paler, but the most certain way of sexing is the constant singing of the cocks.

Pied

This was the first colour mutation to appear in Cockatiels; it was reported in 1949 from two unconnected sources in the USA. The colour pattern is very variable, with the most evenly marked always most sought after, especially if most of the feathers are primrose yellow.

Pied Cockatiel

The best marked birds have a horseshoe pattern of grey evenly over both shoulders with clear primrose back, breast, neck, wings and tail feathers. Both cocks and hens have the orange wing patches surrounded by yellow. However, the average markings of a Pied show more grey; often included in the tail feathers, but the flight feathers should be white or primrose. Often faces will be sooty, and some birds can have a grey band across the chest. Some birds offered as Pieds are mainly grey with a few white blotches; these are more likely to be splits. With splits an occasional bunch of white feathers can occur. There is no reliable way in which the feather patterns identify the sex. Hens will often sing for a short time when young, but this soon ceases; it is the cocks who sing constantly.

Whitefaced
This recessive mutation was first established in Europe in the 1970s. It has no orange cheek patches or any yellow colour. The whole face is white and the eyes are very dark. The wings carry a white stripe as in Normals.

Combined mutations
From the combining and breeding of the various colour mutations come some of the most beautiful and most sought-after Cockatiels.

Cinnamon-Pearl
Cinnamon takes the place of grey in this Pearl mutation. There is a wide range of colours: some are Cinnamon with white pearling or lacing; others, and the more beautiful ones, are Cinnamon with primrose yellow pearling on the shoulders, back and sometimes on the front as well. Cinnamon lacewings are very attractive birds carrying a lot of primrose colour. The crest is Cinnamon streaked with yellow. The hens retain their colours, but the cocks revert, usually after the first moult, to a very pretty soft light grey.

Cinnamon-Pearl Cockatiel hen

Cinnamon-Pied

This is like the Pied with the grey of the Pied replaced with the softer cinnamon colour. The cocks are often darker than the hens, sometimes with a marbled effect.

Cinnamon-Pied Cockatiel

Cinnamon-Pearl-Pied Cockatiel hen

Cinnamon-Pearl-Pied
The cinnamon colour can range from light to dark, the pied from white to an overall deep primrose. They can be pearled or Lacewing, the amount of which varies. The most sought after have clear primrose fronts, back, wings and tail feathers.

Pearl Pied

This is the same colour as the Pied but with pearling, or it can be a Lacewing. The hens retain the pearling, but at the moult the cocks lose theirs and revert to looking like a Pied. Some cocks take one or two years to revert, so the only sure way to sex is to listen for the continual singing of the cocks.

Pearl Pied Cockatiels

Lutino-Pearl Cockatiels

Lutino-Pearl

This mutation is starting to overtake the popularity of the Lutino. The primrose to golden pearling is retained in maturity by the hens, so this is the most yellow looking of cockatiels. The cocks revert to a plain white or primrose colour at the moult, looking just like a Lutino, but they do not acquire the lavender wash down the back.

Choosing and buying

Choosing a pet cockatiel, or the right pair for an aviary, is always a pleasure and a little thought on the subject will be well repaid in future years. Cockatiels have been known to live as long as 27 years, although a more average lifespan would be about 15 years. They breed well for up to 10 or 12 years.

The worst thing a prospective pet owner can do is to just go out and buy a Cockatiel at random. That way leads to disappointment for the owner and often a life of misery for the bird.

Anyone buying a pet Cockatiel should always ensure that it is a very young bird. Adults who have passed their breeding prime and been shunted off to a pet shop should not be bought as pets. Either cocks or hens who have been used to aviary life with a partner, and perhaps producing young for several years, will not be contented with a solitary life in a cage. Adult birds suddenly confined to cage life, even if they are out for most of the day, will get very frustrated and, even if they become tame, are liable to bite their owner's fingers. An angry or frightened adult Cockatiel can give quite a nasty bite.

All Cockatiels are individuals; it is of the greatest importance to get a bird which suits the owner. Nervous young birds do not make good pets for young people, who may not have sufficient patience and understanding of the fears of the baby bird. Cockatiels are not suitable pets for very young children. They may pick the bird up and if it is tame and does not bite, may hold it far too hard, quite literally squeezing it to death.

People who want a Cockatiel who will learn to talk should never buy a hen: it is extremely rare for a hen Cockatiel to talk, but quite usual for cocks, although some develop a lovely song instead. Our own pet Cockatiel does not say a word but is a tremendous character, and has a varied and beautiful song. Some people enjoy the more gentle and confiding nature of hens.

Many breeders of cockatiels find it easier to dispose of their unwanted and young stock to pet shops and bird farms, and many very nice birds of various colours and mutations can be bought from these establishments.

When buying, either directly from the breeder or from a shop, look for a bright-eyed bird which is active and alert. Birds with a sleepy appearance are best avoided, even though the cause may be lack of sleep if they are in a shop. Birds seen in aviaries should be active, moving and above all flying well. Avoid a bird which climbs everywhere in an aviary; its mode of transport should be its wings. It does not matter if the tail feathers are dirty, but the vent must be clean and dry.

Avoid all birds with sharp protruding breast bones. The birds should rest on a perch with two claws one side and two claws on the other side of the perch. Wings should not be drooping unless a bird is in an aviary and very wet, when it will spread its wings to dry them. Normally the wings rest across the rump of the bird.

A healthy cockatiel, even when nervous or out of breath from flying, should not emit any 'choky', 'wheezing' sounds. The nostrils should be quite dry and the eyes bright and free of any discharge. The feathers of a healthy bird lie smooth and flat on its body; a 'fluffed up' bird may just be very cold or it may have something wrong internally.

A bird's tail is its rudder and if it has lost all its tail feathers it cannot fly properly, and will climb about. These take at least two to three months to grow again, which in the case of breeding pairs often means a breeding season lost. Birds intended for an aviary should never be put into a strange new home late at night. Keep them in a cage overnight with food and water and put them in their new quarters in daytime. Before letting them go, show them the food and water, and make sure they do not hang on the wire of a flight the first night. Even if a cat or fox cannot reach them, they can and do break their necks dashing about in the dark if disturbed in a strange new home.

Housing

Pet cages for the household

To keep a happy and contented Cockatiel in your home it is vital to have the right size and sort of cage. A pet Cockatiel is quite different from other pet birds, such as budgerigars. It needs more space, it needs to spend as much time as possible outside its cage and to be allowed to fly around.

When siting the cage in the house it must be out of reach of cats and dogs, and be positioned out of draughts. It is essential to cover over part of the cage at night with a piece of dark coloured material, so that the bird can sleep while the lights are on. A word of warning: if kept in a kitchen, be careful not to burn a teflon coated pan, as the fumes from this type of pan burning are poisonous.

Size and shape

Most cages for budgerigars and canaries are not big enough for a cockatiel, which likes to stretch and flap its wings. If an ornamental cage is not required, the illustrated standard plywood breeding cage is ideal. This is about 25 cm wide, 60 cm long and 45 cm high (10 × 24 × 18 inches). They are available at very modest prices from nearly all pet shops and should have pull-out metal trays for easy cleaning. If an ornamental cage is required, there is a wide range of types and prices available. Shape is important, and it is better to be rectangular, as shown in the illustration, than high with a small base, because it is natural for cockatiels to walk about on the floor.

Equipment

Mirrors, swings and ladders are unnecessary.

One or two perches at the most are sufficient. They should be made of wood no more than 125 mm ($\frac{1}{2}$ inch) in diameter.

Tube type drinkers and feeders are unsuitable for cockatiels, which are much happier with open clip-on

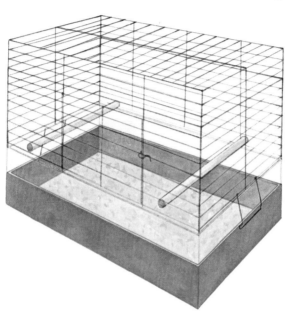

Ideal form of cage for a pet cockatiel, which requires much more space than other pet birds, such as the budgerigar

feeding and drinking utensils inside the cage. Food and water containers need to be much bigger than those for budgies and canaries.

Aviaries

Many people will be attracted to the idea of keeping cockatiels out of doors, either a pair with the interest and excitement of breeding or maybe more than one pair on a colony system.

Positioning

Although they are not considered noisy birds, the cocks do sing and call for some periods during the day. When deciding on the position of the aviary, consideration should be given to neighbours. The birds like a sunny position and they should not be exposed to cold, wet and windy conditions.

Dimensions

Before buying or making an aviary carefully consider your requirement, as a wrong decision can lead to problems and frustration later. The minimum size required for one pair of birds should be a house or shelter 1 × 1 × 2 metres (3 × 3 × 6 feet) high with the adjoining flight a metre wide and 3 metres long (3 × 9 feet).

If you propose to breed cockatiels, the day will arrive when you may have to remove the young from too confined a space if the parents are to be allowed to go to nest again.

If some are to be kept, more space will be needed. So when choosing your aviary flexibility is important. Look for one that can easily be extended. For an aviary to keep two pairs of birds the house size can be the same as for a single pair, but the flight needs to be larger, 2 × 3 metres (6 × 9 feet).

To keep a colony of four pairs of birds, and have plenty of space for their young, a small summerhouse in a corner can be a most charming feature. The house should be about 2.5 × 2 metres (8 × 6 feet) and with flight panels fitted in a semi-circle, extending to a safety porch at one side of the house, a large flight area is provided.

All our aviary flights are now wider than 1 metre (3 feet) as it was found that in this width the birds would fly away when the flight was entered. With the width increased to a minimum of 1.25 metres (4 feet) the birds would stay steady on a longitudinal perch and become much more tame.

Flooring and roofing

Grass or gravel flooring is not satisfactory, as it will be difficult to keep clean to maintain the birds in a healthy condition, and after a time the ground would have to be dug up and replaced. A more simple way to make a base than shuttering and laying concrete is to use paving stones, which are available in a range of sizes at garden centres.

The roofs of flights will need some covering. Aviaries have been known to blow over in severe gales, so it is prudent to fix both house and flight to the base.

Above: *Typical colony aviary ideal for Cockatiels*
Below: *Standard small attractive aviary ideal for two pairs of cockatiels*

Equipment

Perches should be made from 15 mm ($\frac{5}{8}$ inch) diameter dowelling and should be fitted higher in the house than in the flight, as birds usually go to the highest perch at night. Natural branches can also be used, such as

hazelnut, apple or beech; do not use hawthorn, silver birch or oak, as they can be injurious. Leave plenty of free space for flying in the flight and put the perches the length of the flight, not crossways.

A water container should be placed on the floor of the flight. Ideally it should be rectangular, 75 mm (3 inches) deep, made of plastic, of the sort that can be found in garden centres.

Lighting is not essential, but is a great benefit in case of 'night frights'. It will also give extended feeding time in the winter. Dimmers and time switches are luxuries both owners and birds will enjoy, but take care that all the electric wiring is external or protected, not exposed to the birds who would certainly chew them.

Brushing or rolling black bitumastic paint on both sides of the flight wiring has a double benefit, as apart from helping to preserve the wire, the owner can more clearly see the birds, and they can see out more clearly themselves than through shiny wire.

Flight tops should be covered with clear or opaque plastic sheets to give protection. Removable sheets should be fitted to keep out the cold, wet and wind on the weather sides in the winter.

Creosote should not be used to preserve woodwork; it can be injurious to the birds. The preservatives Bio-Woody or Cuprinol are recommended.

Security

It is essential to have a safety porch so that birds do not escape when the aviary is entered. Many aviaries have low doors, based on a theory that the birds fly high. This may well work for a lot of the time, but birds do sometimes fly low and escape. If this does happen, the chances of retrieving a cockatiel are very remote.

If there is likely to be a problem with cats or foxes double wire is most certainly recommended, as many a bird has been maimed or destroyed when flying on to the wire after being panicked at night, and been caught by a marauder's claws. The extra layer of wire outside will prevent such tragedies, which happen all too often.

Inside an aviary 'house'. Of particular importance are the feeding shelf (right) and roosting perch (centre)

General care

Very young Cockatiels (6 to 9 weeks old) are best with a paper floor covering. Wipe newspaper thoroughly before using; excess newsprint is poisonous to birds. The paper needs to be changed at least once a day. On this floor should be spread a little mixed grit, grated or scraped cuttlefish bone, a little oystershell grit and a little finely cut up lettuce and cabbage, with some grated carrot. Next sprinkle some small seeds such as canary and mixed millets and, if possible, some sunflower kernels which have been slightly crushed. Then sprinkle some crumbled bread and milk and a little moistened and crumbled egg rearing food over the floor. All this must of course be renewed every day. Gradually the bird will get used to eating food from containers, just as it has to learn to drink from a container. Greenfood, carrots, etc. can later be wedged in the bars of the cage, fresh daily. Cuttlefish bone can also be wedged in the bars. The feeding requirements for a pet are almost exactly the same as for birds kept in aviaries outdoors.

An important aspect of general care is to keep the aviary clean. Excreta, seed husks and dust should be cleared up at least once a week, daily if possible. Water and seed should be supplied fresh daily and containers kept clean. This means blowing or sweeping away seed husks, turning out the container, and adding fresh seed. The dust which collects *daily* at the bottom of seed trays is a source of germs, and spores of fungus in hot damp summer weather can cause many health problems.

Perches should be cleaned regularly with a wet cloth soaked in a weak solution of one of the disinfectants available for birds. This saves a lot of eye infections. Houses should be washed or thoroughly sprayed with a good aviary disinfectant at least twice a year.

The cages for Cockatiels of all ages should be partly covered with dark material at night, so that the bird is not disturbed by lights. Never leave a cage in a draught,

When choosing a young bird as a pet, it must be active but with patience they can be trained to perch on a finger

not even on a hot summer's day; and never leave it within reach of a cat.

Pet Cockatiels greatly appreciate a twice weekly spray with a plant sprayer. They need plenty of daily exercise, but do remember that any bird, no matter how young, or how tame, will fly straight out of an open door or window, and since they fly very fast and very straight, they are out of their home area in seconds. The chances of recovery are often not very good.

Toys, swings, mirrors etc. are not for Cockatiels.

What they most like is affection and to have their heads stroked, the way the feathers grow. Something which all Cockatiels, wherever they are, and especially those living in the house, enjoy very much is a twice weekly supply of small twigs of willow, hazel nut, or apple, well washed and with the leaves removed, but not the buds.

Training

Taming

Training young Cockatiels is not difficult, but it does require some patience, especially with a nervous bird. Do not attempt any training for the first few days, but get the bird eating well and accustomed to its surroundings first. Then start by putting a hand palm downwards on the perch beside its feet. If it panics, remove your hand and try again later. If it does not, it is steady and will progress quickly.

The next step is to ease your fingers under the bird's feet, move it away from the perch, and then back. Next try to get the bird to stay on the back of your hand while it is removed from the cage. When it finds itself outside the cage it will probably panic and fly into the nearest window (draw the curtains first!). If this happens rub its head, console it and return it to the cage. Two such sessions a day are enough for a baby bird. Once used to being out it will soon learn by trial and error to fly round and round a room.

The next step is to shoulder train the bird; put it on your shoulder, talking to it all the time, then put it down on some suitable place, and call it by its name; it will soon learn to come to the shoulder after it has flown round and round a room.

Training to talk

When teaching it to talk, speak clearly, not too fast, and with medium volume. Names ending in y or ie, such as Joey, Andy, Bobby etc. are usually fairly easy for a young bird, but some names are very difficult for birds, such as Harry and Philip. Keep addressing the bird by its name, then add words of praise. Many of our aviary birds say 'very good' simply because they hear me say these words to them.

Feeding

A plentiful variety of foods, and really good quality clean, shiny seeds are of the utmost importance when keeping Cockatiels, either pet birds or those in aviaries.

When buying a pet bird for keeping indoors, where at least some of the time it will be in a cage, or for an aviary, ask on what it has been fed. If the answer includes only a very limited number of items, the bird should gradually be encouraged to try different foods so that its diet is really varied. That way the owner will be much more likely to have a happy, healthy and contented pet. Some staff in pet shops know very little about the various birds they are selling, and in any case what will keep a bird alive for a limited period in a shop is very different from what will bring it into the sleek and immaculate good looks which are so admired in well-kept pets or aviary Cockatiels.

Certain foods are absolute necessities for good health, either for pet birds kept in cages or those kept in aviaries.

Seeds

Three seeds form the basic food for Cockatiels: sun-flower seeds, canary seed and mixed millet seeds. A good quality budgie mixture containing rather more mixed millets than canary seeds should make up two-thirds of the seeds offered. The other third should be mixed sunflower seeds. Very young Cockatiels cannot crack the hard sunflower kernels. They learn to do this at about $2\frac{1}{2}$ or 3 months old.

All seeds should be turned out every day, the husks blown away, and any dust thrown out. Sunflower is especially dusty and must be supplied fresh daily.

A seed which is enjoyed by Cockatiels as an extra is clipped oats or its more refined form groats. Half a teaspoon two or three times a week for a pet Cockatiel, and the same quantity per bird in aviaries can be given.

Pet or breeding Cockatiels kept in outdoor aviaries may be given very small quantities of whole hemp seed in extremely cold weather. About six heads per bird per

Collection of feeding utensils for the cage or aviary

day just while the cold weather lasts is good for them. Hemp is a very oily seed and must be in perfect condition. When broken the oil goes rancid and does the birds more harm than good.

Two other oil-containing seeds, linseed and black rape seed, may also be given in tiny quantities in the winter. A very small half teaspoonful per two birds two or three times a week varies their diet. In really miserable weather some sprays of millet will cheer up Cockatiels and give them some occupation.

Containers
Pet bird owners should make sure that containers for both seed and water are large enough for the Cockatiel to get its head in easily without knocking its crest. Excellent containers for seed in aviaries are 13–18 cm (5–7 inch) plastic plant holders.

Grit and minerals
A good quality mixed grit, or mineralized grit, plus oystershell grit, must be supplied fresh daily for a pet living in a cage, or at least twice weekly for birds in aviaries. A Cockatiel will only pick out the bits of grit

which it feels it can swallow comfortably; all the rest will be left, so be sure to renew grit very frequently.

Cuttlefish bone

Calcium is vital to the well-being of all birds, especially so when they are breeding: without sufficient calcium a hen will become egg-bound. The best way to supply calcium is with fresh cuttlefish bone.

It must be clean, white and fresh. Cockatiels will not eat wet or very dirty or brown looking cuttle, which is probably polluted with oil. Wedge a good sized piece through the wires of a pet bird's cage, and drive two small headed nails half way into a wooden upright in an aviary. Make two holes in the bone and spear it on to the nails. Breeding Cockatiels need large quantities of fresh cuttlebone.

A daily supply of fresh vegetables such as carrot and celery is very important

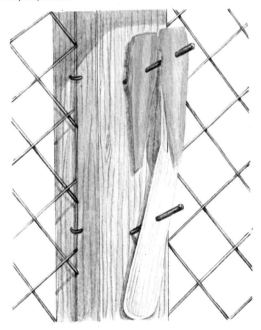

Fresh foods

All Cockatiels, whether they are pet birds in the home, or living in aviaries, must be supplied with daily green food and root vegetables. Cockatiels are not fruit lovers, but some will eat sweet apples. Most of them much prefer wedges of carrot or celery pushed through the bars of their cages or speared onto nails in their flights, in the same manner as for the cuttlefish bone. A daily supply of fresh green salads or vegetable is very important. Spring greens, cabbage, sprouts, broccoli, spinach, lettuce, cress and green celery leaves are all good foods to offer. Whatever is offered must be fresh and green, not yellow or bleached, and very well washed. Cabbage leaves containing slugs or worms could pass on eggs of internal worms, causing great harm to the bird's health.

Many breeders of Cockatiels feed their birds round the year with light brown bread and milk, or in very hot weather bread and water. This means making the bread wet with water and usually milk as well, squeezing it out and crumbling as much as possible. This is given once a day in winter, twice in summer, with the addition of either hard boiled yolk of egg or an egg-rearing food when the birds are breeding.

Wild foods

Many people with access to country areas like to give their birds some of the many excellent wild foods available. But a word of warning is necessary here. Roadside verges in many areas are now sprayed with weed killer. Everywhere farmers and market gardeners are using all kinds of insecticides, some of which would be very poisonous to birds. So it is necessary to use extreme care when gathering wild foods for birds. Even private gardeners, especially rose and chrysanthemum growers, are liable to use many kinds of sprays for their plants, which may drift on to a patch of chickweed they have been growing especially for the birds. Huge heads of sunflower seeds are proudly presented to some bird keepers. It is extremely unwise to let the birds have such delicacies as they may pick up all kinds of fungal spores, plus all the dust collected from a summer in a garden.

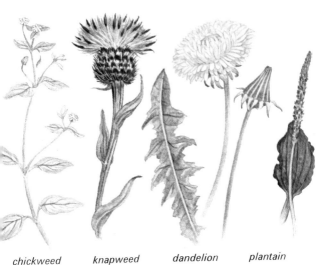

chickweed   *knapweed*   *dandelion*   *plantain*

Those who have access to places where sprays of any kind are not used may like to give their birds dandelion seeding heads, but not the stalks as the juice is too strong for Cockatiels, but very young leaves may be given. Seeding knapweed and its young leaves will be very much enjoyed in the summer. Some people like to feed their birds chickweed but I have found that it shrivels so quickly that Cockatiels tend to leave it alone.

Two garden flowers greatly enjoyed when seeding are the common calendula, and the forget-me-not.

The autumn is a particularly abundant time of year for berries, three of which will be eaten by Cockatiels: hawthorn, but remove the leaves and those terrible spikes; the common wild elderberries, but remember the juice will stain the bird's plumage; and the scarlet berries of the mountain ash or rowan. In all cases the leaves should be removed and the branches and berries washed.

Many people do not realize that there are very many extremely poisonous plants growing in the country-side, and often in their gardens too. Some of the most common are illustrated. Almost every part of yew, so common in churchyards, would be poisonous to Cockatiels. It is not always known that the seeds of that popular garden flowering tree, the laburnum, are extremely poisonous. The dwarf elder is very poisonous

Bark and buds

willow

beech

apple

hazelnut

Wild berries

hawthorn

elderberry

mountain ash

Garden flowers

calendula

forget-me-not

to birds and, unfortunately, many parents and children are unaware that the deadly nightshade is well named: it is fatal to Cockatiels and humans.

Cockatiels kept as pets in the home can be offered little bits from the table such as a tiny piece of cheddar cheese, or a little piece of plain cake or biscuit. But they are not particularly interested in human food.

Bark and buds

One of the biggest treats that can be offered to either caged birds or those which are kept in aviaries is a piece of hazel nut or willow. The leaves should be removed, leaving the buds at the base of the leaves intact, and the whole should be gently washed, taking care not to knock off the buds. The bark and buds of these two trees give immense pleasure to pet Cockatiels. Those in aviaries will very greatly appreciate branches of hazelnut, willow, apple or beech to chew, especially during the autumn, winter and spring months. Do not give breeding birds branches; it is likely to take their attention away from the job in hand, which is breeding!

Tonics

Autumn, winter and spring are the times of year to give tonics to Cockatiels. There are very many excellent ones available at almost any pet shop or establishment selling foods, aviaries etc. for birds. It is necessary to change the seed two or three times per week when using any product containing some of the B complex of vitamins. If allowed to get stale and damp, they can cause harmful fungi to develop on the seeds. Cockatiels benefit very greatly from a prolonged course of tonics containing all or some of the B complex of vitamins. Birds so treated when breeding will be less liable to infertility and also chicks dying before they hatch.

Pet birds kept in the home can benefit greatly from such tonics for a period of about two months at a time, with a rest of three months. If the bird or birds are not eating their seeds the tonic should be discontinued for a few days, and fresh untreated seed given. The tonic may be tried again but with only the slightest trace at first.

Poisonous plants

*deadly night shade (*Atropa Bella-donna*)*

*yew (*Taxus Baccata*)*

*Laburnum (*Laburnum Anagyroides*)*

*dwarf elder (*Sambucus Ebulus*)*

Breeding

The appeal of a nest full of baby Cockatiels, their lovely colours intensified by extreme youth, inspires many pet Cockatiel owners to have an aviary in their garden and, with the aid of one or more breeding pairs of Cockatiels, produce their own versions.

Specialist breeders usually breed one pair to an aviary, but some of these, and increasing numbers of people just keeping a few pairs, and finding that the birds breed better and are much more contented if there are two or even three pairs to a slightly larger flight.

Colonies of four or five pairs make a lovely sight in a large well designed aviary installed as a feature in a garden. For the newcomer to Cockatiel breeding who wants to have a colony of birds, the best plan is to limit the number of pairs to a maximum of four, and to obtain if possible at least two compatible breeding pairs, and two pairs which are either staying together, or if this is not the case, unrelated birds, two of each sex, so that it does not matter how they pair.

Young cocks can breed at 10 months old, young hens at 11 to 12 months old, but it is better to let them get a little older before allowing them to breed.

Cockatiels breeding at around a year old should be stopped from rearing more than two nests of young, or an average of about eight or nine chicks. Older birds may be allowed to rear 10 to 12 young in any one year. Beyond that their strength is likely to be very much overtaxed. There is only one way to stop some Cockatiels from breeding themselves to exhaustion: remove all the nest boxes.

Colour combinations

Before deciding what colours to have, bear in mind certain genetic rules regarding pairing. If a Normal (grey) bird of either sex is put with any of the Pied mutations, the resultant young will all be grey birds, split for various colours. Split means that the bird carries the colour without displaying it, but paired to

Lutino-Pearl Cockatiel Chicks

the right partner can produce offspring displaying the colour.

A Lutino mated with any of the Pied mutations will also produce grey young. Before deciding on the colours to be introduced to a colony aviary it would be as well to study the chapter on colours in this book, and to seek the advice of specialist breeders.

If you pair a Normal bird with any Pied mutation the young will all be grey birds split for various colours

Nothing is more disappointing for the newcomer to Cockatiels than to spend time and money on building aviaries and buying perhaps individually beautiful birds, only to find they breed Normal looking young (grey) because genetically it was impossible for them to do anything else.

Equipment

Nest boxes for adult breeding Cockatiels can be put up in early spring, or a little later in cold situations.

A good Cockatiel nest box, which can be bought at pet shops and bird farms is approximately 20 × 22 × 35 cm (8 × 9 × 14 inches) deep, with a removable lid. This is much safer than a hinged one, which can fall back on your hand as chicks are being removed for inspection or ringing.

A ladder is necessary to enable the young to climb out; if one is not built into the box, a piece of wood 4 cm (1½ inches) square with steps cut into it can be screwed from the outside into one front corner of the box. It should reach to level with the entrance hole. The entrance hole for modern mutation Cockatiels needs to be large, 65 mm (2½ inches) in diameter.

Bark is not recommended for nesting material. Some breeders use wood shavings. Sawdust is not good; it can be picked up by the young birds and tiny pieces of sharp wood can pierce their crops. An excellent material is dry brown Irish peat moss, and in cold spring weather it can have a thin topping of compressed pet litter, but be sure there are no chemicals in this material.

The nesting material should be put into the box to a depth of about 13 cm (5 inches). About half way through a breeding season always look to see if a wooden ladder has been worn smooth by parents amusing themselves with chewing sessions. In this case it will be useless for the young and the level of the nesting material must be brought up to 5 cm (2 inches) from the base of the entrance hole, otherwise the young may find it impossible to leave the nest.

Nest box, showing ideal position of the 'ladder'

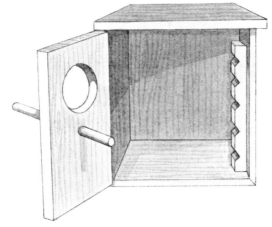

Breeding Cockatiels need a large container of water about 4 cm (1½ inches) deep, in which to bath; they go wet into the nest box to add humidity to the eggs at a certain time.

Laying, incubation and hatching

The usual clutch of eggs is between four and six, but young hens sometimes lay more. Any over six are best removed to avoid placing too great a strain on the parents feeding hungry mouths for several weeks. Clear eggs look pinkish, fertile eggs look cloudy and almost grey.

Newcomers are always surprised to find that the cock does a lot of the brooding with breeding Cockatiels. With experienced pairs the cock sits during the day, the hen at night; sometimes they sit together for long periods if it is very cold, or when the chicks are hatching. Inexperienced parents do all sorts of things, but they learn during the first year.

The eggs take 17 to 21 days to hatch. The chicks have fluff at first but soon lose this and are bare, with closed eyes until on the eighth to tenth day the eyes begin to open.

Dead in shell chicks, which for some reason have failed to hatch, should always be removed as soon as possible. Also any young which have been accidentally crushed. Do not force the parents aside for this operation. They will step aside when they are ready for the owner to remove eggs etc.

Always whistle or talk to breeding Cockatiels on the nest when approaching and interfere as seldom as possible, especially with young birds. Do not be tempted to disturb parents who are hatching chicks, or have very tiny babies; they may crush them if disturbed.

Chicks' development and care

The young benefit greatly in cold weather from at least one infertile egg, left as a hot water bottle. It can be removed when the chicks have pin feathers: i.e. when the feathers are still little rolled up spikes resembling a short thick pin. The rate of growth varies greatly. Some pin feathers appear at two weeks, quickly followed by opened feathers, until by four weeks the bird is fully feathered and ready to leave the nest. Others take longer and wait until about five weeks before launching themselves into the world.

When a young Cockatiel leaves the nest, whether it is a very forward one in hot weather at three to four weeks of age, or whether it is the more usual time of around five weeks, it is best to return it to its nest for the first night, but only if it is known from which nest it came.

If closed ringing is to be done, it must be carried out as soon as the chick's feet are large enough to hold the ring.

Group of young cockatiels in a towel-lined bowl

Close ringing of baby birds is not something which most people progressing from keeping one or more pet birds indoors to an outdoor aviary will be likely to undertake. It is a tricky little operation, requiring some practice. If it must be done, do be very sure to tell the ringmakers whether the birds are Normals, or are Mutation Cockatiels. If the birds are any colour other than grey, the chances are that their legs, when they grow up, will be very short and very thick. This means that a much bigger ring must be used.

Close ringing is done when the ring can be slipped over the three largest toes, up to the knuckle of the foot and as far as it will go over the smallest toe, then with a sharpened matchstick pull the smallest toe through the ring. This operation usually has to be done at about ten days old. After a few days a closed ring cannot be removed except under anaesthetic by a veterinary surgeon.

Young chicks need soft food. Light brown bread moistened with cold water and then dunked in some milk, squeezed out and crumbled, with a little yolk of hard boiled egg crumbled on top is excellent. It must be changed daily, twice a day in hot weather.

When young birds leave the nest they usually fly straight onto the wire of the flight, and hang there helplessly, the prey to the first passing cat. At this time it is particularly necessary to have double wiring with a gap between the layers, so that predators cannot reach the baby birds.

Lower the level of water to about 2 cm ($\frac{3}{4}$ inch) and put a small flat stone at one end of the container, so that chicks coming out of the nest do not fall into the water and drown. Young birds begging for food from their parents after the age of six weeks are best removed, for their own good and that of the parents.

Parents anxious to go back to nest sometimes feather pluck their young, in which case spray them with an anti-feather plucking aerosol. Take each chick out, shield its eyes carefully, and spray according to instructions twice daily. Usually the feathers will grow again quite fast when the young learn to feed themselves, which they tend to do very quickly when suffering from such parents.

Breeding diet

An additional aid to breeding parent Cockatiels is any good egg rearing food. This can be put on top of the bread and milk, in place of the egg yolk, and should be supplied fresh, twice per day. Soft food must, of course, be given in a separate container from seeds.

Many Cockatiels feed their young huge quantities of

Parent feeding one of its young

dry sunflower kernels. Always give a twice daily supply of mixed sunflower seeds to breeding birds. The dust from the husks is plentiful, so it really must be changed twice a day. Sunflower should be fed in a separate container, but canary and millet seeds can be mixed together. Soaked seed used to be fed to Cockatiels as a matter of course; now most of them prefer the above foods. Those who wish to try this food for their birds should soak canary and millet seed for 24 hours, put it into a sieve and wash thoroughly, drain away as much water as possible, and feed twice a day. It goes sour very quickly and also dries out very fast, then the birds leave it alone.

Ailments

Worms and stress are probably the two most common causes of illness in Cockatiels. They are intelligent, affectionate, and nervous if upset, with a somewhat similar temperament in certain ways to that of Cockatoos.

Protection, no overcrowding, and cleanliness will work wonders.

Worms
Cockatiels living indoors, if bought very young, are not likely to suffer from worms; newly acquired adults are another matter. Cockatiels and all parrot-type birds can suffer from internal worms when kept in aviaries, and can die if not treated. There are three kinds of worms

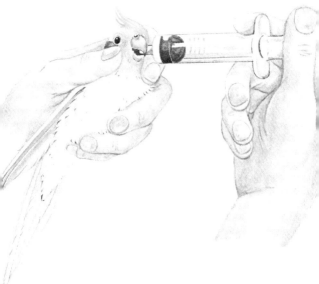

The best way to worm a cockatiel is to use a syringe. This shows the most effective way of holding the bird

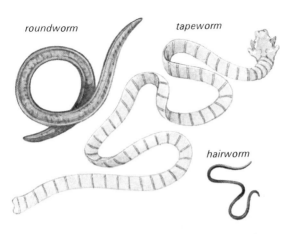

roundworm

tapeworm

hairworm

Three kinds of worms from which Cockatiels are likely to suffer

from which Cockatiels are likely to suffer – tapeworms, roundworms (*ascaridia*) and hair worms (*cappilaria*). The two last are the most common; roundworms are small and white and may be seen if expelled.

There are many kinds of medicine available. Two points to remember: do *not* use children's worm remedies, only those especially made for animals and birds. Do not expect complete destruction of all worms and eggs if a preparation is put in the drinking water. Cockatiels can go two or three days without water if the weather is not hot.

With a collection of birds in an aviary, far the better way is to give the worm medicine by means of a syringe into the mouth and over the tongue. The experts use various attachments to the syringe so that a 'tube' goes down the throat; this is not necessary as the chances of the liquid getting on the lungs is very slight: the bird automatically 'closes' that passage when it feels the nozzle of a syringe in its mouth. If the bird blows back some of the liquid via its nostrils, give it a tiny drop more.

Do not worm before the age of eight weeks; it is best to do the worming in the spring and autumn and not when the birds are breeding.

Some people may not wish to worm their birds individually; there are some very good preparations especially for birds, which can be put in the water.

Mites

Occasionally feather-eating mites attack both aviary and pet birds. Anti-mite aerosol products are available to combat these pests.

The little grey mite which lives in wood crevices, and comes out at night to suck birds' blood, called red mite (it looks red when full of blood at night) can weaken both adults and young birds so much that serious illness can result.

Pet shops and bird farms are full of products, many of them in aerosol form, to combat problems with all kinds of mites.

Mosquitoes and gnats can also attack and worry birds a great deal in summer. It is a good idea to spray underneath all nest boxes every evening in the summer with an anti-mite aerosol which discourages mosquitoes from attacking baby birds in the nest. If possible, try either to do away with compost heaps, or site them well away from aviaries. They are a terrible

Cockatiels may suffer from feather-eating insects

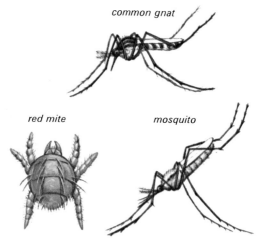

common gnat

red mite   *mosquito*

source of mosquitoes and gnats. In the UK spiders should be encouraged to set up home in aviaries as they do an excellent job, destroying all kinds of insects. At the end of the breeding season nest boxes should be soaked for 48 hours in a dustbin filled with water and a liberal quantity of any powerful disinfectant, then rinsed, dried and stored in a dry place.

Egg binding

An egg-bound hen may still be eating but its eyes may be closed and it may be on the floor of the aviary or cage. Pick it up in a gloved hand so that it can happily bite the glove during examination. Feel round and below the area of the vent; if it feels full and there is a lump, it is very likely an egg.

Put the bird in a cage with three sides and a roof (a single breeder cage) place on a piece of warm towel and put the cage on a chair in front of an electric fire – not too close; the temperature should be about 27°C (80°F). If a hospital cage is used, remember the floor temperature may be far above that registered on the thermometer. Do not let the floor temperature go above 27°C (80°F). Give the bird half a teaspoon ($\frac{3}{4}$ ml) of lukewarm (boiled) water with a big pinch of glucose or sugar mixed into it every three hours.

Extremely gentle pressure may be applied from both sides downwards towards the vent, but stop immediately if the bird protests or shows any signs of stress. If an egg is laid, keep the bird warm and with seed and water until she shows signs of wanting to return to her aviary. If no egg is laid within 24 hours, take the bird in a warm box to a veterinary practitioner.

Eye infections

Cockatiels are very prone to minor eye infections, which can sometimes be no more than dust in the eye. Clean the eye with lukewarm water, and a very soft handkerchief. Never use cotton buds or any kind of cotton wool as the tiny strands get into the eye and cause untold trouble. If the problem does not clear up, the bird must be taken to a vet who will probably prescribe an antibiotic cream. Put a tiny quantity on the lower lid of the eye and remember to wash the eye gently each time before a fresh application of ointment is given. It is usual to give such treatment for five days, then rest the bird for five days. When returning the bird to a cage or aviary, be sure that the perches are well washed and kept very clean.

More serious eye complaints, when the corner of the eye is dark pink or red, can be a sign of many infections, and a vet must be consulted. When giving antibiotics it is advisable to give about half a millilitre ($\frac{1}{4}$ teaspoon) of plain yoghourt once a day two hours before giving the antibiotic. This replaces the flora in the intestines. It is usual to give internal antibiotics for five days, then rest the bird, and repeat the medication five days later if necessary.

Burns and scalds

A victim of burning, or scalding water, should be immediately rushed to a running cold water tap, and drenched for a few seconds, especially the head, eyes and feet. If this is done very quickly it will lessen the burning or scalding. Gently dry the bird and give it one or two beakfuls of lukewarm water and glucose, or sugar, $\frac{1}{8}$ teaspoon of either to one tablespoon of lukewarm water. Next put it on some soft material on the floor of its cage, and keep in a warm place if the weather is cold. Repeat the sips of glucose or sugar and water two hours later, and again if necessary. Give the bird some soft food such as bread and milk and egg food.

Haemorrhaging vent

If a pet bird has a haemorrhage from the vent, it may have picked up some object which it cannot pass. Try half a teaspoon of liquid medicinal paraffin. If it is not better in a few hours, take it to the vet.

Tight rings

Any bird with such a ring which holds its leg up or appears to be in pain should be seen by a vet. Intense pain can be caused by rings which are too small, or as sometimes happens with plastic rings, the bird's leg literally grows round the ring. In such a case, take it to a vet, and get it removed under anaesthetic.

*A group of Pied
Cockatiels showing what
healthy alert birds should
look like*

Rickets

Some Cockatiels which have been bred in over-
crowded conditions, or allowed to breed beyond their
strength, or who have been without sufficient sunlight,
calcium and vitamin A, may be suffering from rickets.
These birds climb rather than fly, and tend to sit on their
legs, not stand on their feet. A vet may be able to help,
but it would be most unwise to breed from such birds.

A bird with closed eyes and watery nostrils, breath-
ing heavily, perhaps with some tail movement, should
be taken to the vet immediately as it could have various
diseases.

Useful addresses

Cage and Aviary Birds (weekly bird magazine),
Prospect House, 9-13 Ewell Road, Cheam, Sutton,
Surrey SM1 4QQ. Telephone: 01-661 4491.

The National Council for Aviculture, 87 Winn Road,
Lee, London SE12 9EY. Telephone: 01-857 4208.

The Parrot Society, 19A De Parys Avenue, Bedford,
Bedfordshire MK40 2TX. Telephone: 0234 58922.
(Membership includes people who keep all types of
parrots and parakeets.)

Oaklands Park Farm Aviaries, Newdigate, nr.
Dorking, Surrey. Telephone: 029 384 408.
(Cages, aviaries, equipment, seeds, books and
birds.)

Southern Aviaries, Tinkers Lane, Hadlow Down,
East Sussex TH22 4EU. Telephone: 082 585 283.
(Cages, aviaries, equipment, seeds, books and
birds.)

There are very many excellent establishments all
over the UK selling the above items. For addresses,
consult *Cage and Aviary Birds*.

Index

Photographic acknowledgements
Dennis Avon 16, 21; Dulcie and Freddie Cooke 11, 12, 17, 19, 20, 22, 23, 47; Cyril Laubscher front cover

Illustrations by Linden Artists Ltd (Steve Lings)